When The Cheers Stop

How to help athletes deal with depression

Dejon Jernagin

When The Cheers Stop

March 2023

ISBN: 9798377547570

Published by
The Man Up Foundation
www.themanupfoundation.com

Printed in the United States of America

Meet Dejon Jernagin . . .

Dejon Jernagin is a dynamic leader who wears many hats as a pastor, business owner, speaker and family man.

He is the pastor of The Transparent Truth Apostolic Ministries, where he is known for his transparency, honesty and commitment to spreading the truth of the Gospel. In addition to his ministry, Dejon is also the president and founder of The Man up Foundation, an organization that helps men develop their leadership skills and reach their full potential.

He is also the owner of California Recruits Scholarship Service, a company that provides scholarships and resources to student athletes.

Dejon's passion for empowering and inspiring others extends beyond his ministry and businesses. He is a certified speaker for the John Maxwell Team, where he shares his expertise and insights on leadership, personal growth, and success with audiences around the world.

But above all, Dejon is a proud husband, father, brother and grandfather. He is dedicated to his family and values the relationships he has with his loved ones.

He is known for his kindness, generosity, and his unwavering commitment to those he loves. In all that he does, Dejon Jernagin embodies the spirit of excellence, integrity, and compassion. He is a true leader and role model for all who know him.

Table of Contents

Foreword

By Keith C. Wolaridge

Athletics have the power to bring people together and inspire us all. But what happens when the cheers stop and the athlete is left to face the reality of life outside of the sport they once dominated? This is a question that many athletes struggle with, and it can be especially difficult for those who have dedicated their entire lives to their sport.

In "What Do You Do When All The Cheers Stop: How Athletes Deal with Depression," Dejon Jernagin explores the challenges that athletes face as they transition from their athletic careers to the next phase of their lives. Through his own personal story and those of other athletes, Dejon sheds light on the realities of depression and the struggle to find meaning and purpose outside of sports.

This book is a must-read for anyone who has been touched by athletics, whether as a player, coach, or fan. It provides valuable insights and lessons for anyone navigating the challenges of change and and transition, and offers a roadmap for finding joy and fulfillment in the face of adversity. So let us join Dejon on this journey as he shares his story and offers a message of hope and inspiration to all athletes.

******

Foreword

By: Candace Armstrong
Mother of Struggling Track Athlete

In this foreword, I am honored to introduce you to, "When The Cheers Stop: How To Help Athletes Deal with Depression." This book is a heartfelt and powerful exploration of the challenges that athletes face when their careers come to an end, and the depression that often accompanies this transition. As an athlete myself,

I know first-hand the joy and fulfillment that comes from competing at a high level, but I also know the challenges of adjusting to life after sports. When the cheers stop, it can be a difficult and lonely journey, and it is often only then that athletes are forced to confront their true feelings and emotions.

This book is a testament to the strength and resilience of athletes, and it is my hope that it will provide comfort, support, and guidance to those who are facing similar challenges. Whether you are an athlete who is transitioning from your athletic career, or someone who is supporting someone who is, this book is for you.

Through a series of personal stories and expert insights, "When the Cheers Stop" provides a compassionate and understanding voice to those who are struggling. The book is organized into ten chapters, each of which explores a different aspect of the athletic experience, from managing expectations and learning to embrace failure, to finding new passions and killing regret.

At its core, "When the Cheers Stop" is a call to action, encouraging athletes to take control of their mental health and well-being. By sharing the stories of athletes who have faced depression and come out on the other side, this book offers hope and inspiration to anyone who is facing life's challenges.

I am grateful to the author, Dejon Jernagin, for writing this book, and for their courage and dedication in bringing this important topic to light. I hope that "When the Cheers Stop" will be a source of comfort, support, and inspiration for athletes everywhere, and that it will help to break the stigma surrounding depression and mental health. ******

Prologue

"When All The Cheers Stop: How Athletes Deal With Depression" is a book written by Dejon Jernagin. The book delves into the topic of depression among athletes and how they deal with it.

The book explores the impact of high-pressure sports environments, intense physical demands, and other stressors that can lead to depression. It also covers the ways in which athletes cope with these challenges, including therapy, medication, and other forms of support.

"Cheers" provides insight into the challenges athletes face and offers hope and support to those who are struggling with depression. The book aims to help athletes understand that they are not alone and that there is a path forward, regardless of how tough the journey may be.

Chapter 1

Managing Expectations

Managing Expectations

Being an athlete is not just about physical training and performance, it also involves managing the mental and emotional stress that comes with the pressure to succeed. In this chapter, we will explore the high expectations that athletes face and how this can lead to depression and other mental health issues.

The Expectations Game

Athletes are often expected to perform at the highest level, both on and off the field, and this can be overwhelming and exhausting. The pressure to win, maintain a certain image, and meet the expectations of fans, coaches, and teammates can take a toll on an athlete's mental and emotional well-being. The need to constantly prove oneself and meet the expectations of others can lead to feelings of anxiety, stress, and even depression.

The Impact of Social Media and the News Cycle

The 24/7 news cycle and the prevalence of social media platforms have only magnified the scrutiny that athletes face. Any mistake or misstep can be quickly spread and analyzed, and the constant barrage of negative comments and criticism can be damaging to an athlete's mental health. In addition, social media can create unrealistic expectations, as athletes are often portrayed as superhuman and indestructible, which can be impossible to live up to.

The Importance of Managing Expectations

To combat the negative impact of expectations, it is essential for athletes to understand that they are human and that it is okay to struggle. It is also important for athletes to set realistic goals and be kind to themselves. This means accepting that setbacks are a normal part of the process and that progress takes time. By setting achievable goals and being mindful of the expectations placed on them, athletes can better manage their mental and emotional well-being.

Seeking Support

In addition to managing expectations, seeking support is also critical in dealing with depression and other mental health issues. No one should have to suffer in silence, and it is important for athletes to know that there is always help available. This can include talking to friends and family, seeking support from mental health professionals, or joining support groups. By reaching out for help, athletes can find the strength and support they need to overcome their struggles and find happiness and fulfillment.

In conclusion, managing expectations is key to preventing depression and other mental health issues in athletes. By setting realistic goals, seeking support, and being kind to oneself, athletes can overcome the challenges they face and achieve their full potential.

The Parents' Role

In addition to the athletes themselves, the role of parents in managing expectations cannot be overstated. Parents play a critical role in shaping their children's understanding of success and in helping them navigate the challenges that come with being an athlete. In this section, we will explore the role of parents in managing expectations and how they can help their children deal with the pressure to succeed.

Setting Realistic Expectations

Parents can set the tone for how their children view success and manage their expectations by setting realistic goals and expectations. This can help their children understand that success is a journey, not a destination, and that setbacks and failures are normal parts of the process. By focusing on effort and progress, rather than just results, parents can help their children develop a more healthy and positive view of success.

Providing Emotional Support

Parents can also provide emotional support to their children by being there for them and listening to their struggles. This means creating a safe and supportive environment where their children feel comfortable discussing their feelings and experiences. By being there for their children, parents can help them overcome their struggles and find the strength and support they need to succeed.

Encouraging Self-Care

In addition to providing emotional support, parents can also help their children manage expectations by encouraging self-care. This can include encouraging their children to take breaks, pursue hobbies, and engage in activities outside of sports. By taking care of their physical and mental well-being, athletes can better manage their expectations and maintain a healthy and positive outlook.

In conclusion, the role of parents in managing expectations is critical to helping athletes overcome the challenges they face. By setting realistic expectations, providing emotional support, and encouraging self-care, parents can help their children develop a healthy and positive view of success and achieve their full potential.

Chapter 2

Losing Vs. Failure

In the world of sports, losing can be a difficult experience, but it is an inevitable part of the process. However, many athletes struggle to differentiate between losing and failure, and this can lead to negative emotions and depression. In this chapter, we will explore the difference between losing and failure, and how understanding this distinction can help athletes overcome the challenges they face.

The Difference Between Losing and Failure

Losing is a temporary setback that occurs when one team or individual does not win a competition. Failure, on the other hand, is a more permanent and negative experience that results from not reaching a goal or not performing to one's own standards. While losing can be disappointing, it is important for athletes to understand that it is not a failure but simply a part of the journey.

The Impact of Losing

Losing can have a significant impact on an athlete's mental and emotional well-being, and it is important for athletes to understand how to manage their emotions and reactions to losing. This can include taking time to reflect on the experience, seeking support from friends and family, and engaging in self-care activities. By managing their emotions and reactions to losing, athletes can better maintain their mental and emotional well-being and avoid the negative impact of depression and other mental health issues.

The Importance of Reframing Failure

Reframing failure as a learning experience, rather than a permanent setback, can also be helpful in overcoming the challenges associated with losing. This means viewing setbacks as opportunities for growth and improvement, and focusing on the progress that has been made, rather than just the results. By reframing failure in this way, athletes can maintain a positive and growth-oriented mindset, and find the strength and resilience they need to overcome their struggles.

In conclusion, understanding the difference between losing and failure is critical in managing expectations and avoiding depression and other mental health issues. By viewing losing as a temporary setback and failure as a learning opportunity, athletes can better manage their emotions and reactions, and maintain a positive and growth-oriented mindset.

Allowing the Loss to Become Your Drive, Not Your End

Losing can be a difficult and emotional experience, but it is important for athletes to understand that it does not have to be the end. Instead, losing can be a source of motivation and drive, propelling athletes to work harder and become better. In this section, we will explore how athletes can use their losses as a source of motivation and turn them into a positive experience.

Finding the Silver Lining

One of the key ways that athletes can turn their losses into a positive experience is by finding the silver lining. This means looking for the positive aspects of the experience, such as the opportunities for growth and improvement, and focusing on the progress that has been made. By finding the silver lining, athletes can maintain a positive outlook and use their losses as a source of motivation.

Learning from Losses

Another way that athletes can use their losses as a source of motivation is by learning from them. This means reflecting on the experience and identifying areas for improvement, and using that knowledge to make changes and become a better athlete. By learning from their losses, athletes can develop a growth mindset and find the motivation they need to continue working hard and improving.

Using Losses as Fuel for Improvement

Finally, athletes can use their losses as fuel for improvement by using the experience as a motivator to work harder and become better. This means using the loss as a catalyst for change, and using the experience to drive progress and improvement. By using their losses as fuel for improvement, athletes can find the motivation they need to overcome their struggles and achieve their goals.

In conclusion, allowing losses to become your drive, rather than your end, is critical in managing expectations and avoiding depression and other mental health issues.

finding the silver lining, learning from losses, and using them as fuel for improvement, athletes can turn their losses into a positive experience and find the motivation they need to succeed.

Chapter 3

Failure Looks Different To a Black Athlete

Cultural Differences with Depression

The experience of depression and mental health issues is not the same for all athletes, and cultural differences can play a significant role.

For Black athletes, the cultural and societal expectations can add an additional layer of pressure and make it harder to cope with failure and depression. In this chapter, we will explore the unique challenges faced by Black athletes and how cultural differences can impact their experience with depression.

The Stigma of Mental Health in the Black Community

The stigma surrounding mental health is a significant issue in many communities, including the Black community. Many Black individuals are not comfortable seeking help for mental health issues, due to the belief that mental illness is a sign of weakness or that they should be able to handle their problems on their own. This stigma can make it harder for Black athletes to cope with depression and other mental health issues, and can prevent them from seeking the help they need.

Cultural Expectations and Pressure

In addition to the stigma surrounding mental health, Black athletes may also face cultural and societal expectations that can add to the pressure they feel. For example, Black athletes may be expected to be strong and resilient, and to handle their problems on their own, which can make it harder for them to cope with failure and depression. This added pressure can make it harder for Black athletes to manage their emotions and expectations, and can lead to negative outcomes for their mental and emotional well-being.

The Need for Support

Despite the challenges they face, it is important for Black athletes to understand that they are not alone and that support is available. This may involve seeking support from family and friends or working with mental health professionals to manage their emotions and expectations. By seeking the help they need, Black athletes can overcome the challenges they face and maintain their mental and emotional well-being.

In conclusion, the cultural differences faced by Black athletes can impact their experience with depression and mental health issues. It is important for Black athletes to understand that they are not alone and that support is available, and to seek the help they need to manage their emotions and expectations. By doing so, Black athletes can overcome the challenges they face and maintain their mental and emotional well-being.

Failure from the White Athlete Perspective

While cultural differences can impact the experience of depression and mental health issues for Black athletes, the experience of white athletes is also not immune to these challenges. In this section, we will explore the challenges faced by white athletes and how they can manage their expectations and cope with failure and depression.

The Pressure of High Expectations

One of the challenges faced by white athletes is the pressure of high expectations. White athletes may feel a strong pressure to succeed and meet expectations, both from themselves and from others. This pressure can make it difficult for white athletes to cope with failure and depression, as they may feel that they have let themselves and others down.

The Impact of Social Comparison

Another challenge faced by white athletes is the impact of social comparison. White athletes may compare themselves to others, and may feel that they are not measuring up. This can lead to feelings of low self-esteem and self-worth, and can make it harder for white athletes to cope with failure and depression.

The Need for Support

Despite the challenges they face, it is important for white athletes to understand that they are not alone and that support is available. This may involve seeking support from family and friends or working with mental health professionals to manage their emotions and expectations. By seeking the help they need, white athletes can overcome the challenges they face and maintain their mental and emotional well-being.

In conclusion, white athletes also face challenges in managing their expectations and coping with failure and depression. It is important for white athletes to understand that they are not alone and that support is available, and to seek the help they need to manage their emotions and expectations. By doing so, white athletes can overcome the challenges they face and maintain their mental and emotional well-being.

"Getting a Division 1 scholarship may be a dream come true for the Black athlete, while going Ivy League may be the goal for the white athlete. Regardless of the path chosen, what truly matters is how the athlete handles the expectations and challenges that come with success and failure. It's not about the destination, but about the journey and the mental and emotional resilience that the athlete builds along the way."

Dejon Jernagin

Chapter 4

Small Victories Outside of Primary Sports

While an athlete's primary sport may define their identity and success, it is important to remember that success can be found in other areas of life as well. In this chapter, we will explore the importance of finding small victories outside of primary sports and how these victories can help athletes maintain their mental and emotional well-being.

The Importance of a Balanced Life

Athletes often put a lot of pressure on themselves to succeed in their primary sport. However, this pressure can take a toll on their mental and emotional well-being, especially when they are faced with failure.

Finding small victories outside of primary sports can help athletes maintain a sense of balance and well-being, and can give them a sense of accomplishment and pride.

Discovering New Passions and Interests

Finding small victories outside of primary sports can also help athletes discover new passions and interests. By exploring new areas of interest, athletes can develop new skills and find a sense of purpose beyond their primary sport. This can provide a sense of fulfillment and can help athletes maintain their mental and emotional well-being, even when faced with challenges in their primary sport.

The Power of Support Systems

Having a strong support system can also play a significant role in helping athletes find small victories outside of primary sports. Support from family and friends can provide encouragement and motivation, and can help athletes maintain their well-being, even in the face of challenges.

In conclusion, finding small victories outside of primary sports can help athletes maintain a sense of balance and well-being. By exploring new passions and interests and having a strong support system, athletes can build resilience and find fulfillment in their lives beyond their primary sport.

The Sport Cannot and Does Not Define Your Person

Athletes often place a great deal of importance on their sport, and may feel that their sport defines their identity and success. However, it is important to remember that the sport does not define who you are as a person. In this section, we will explore the dangers of allowing your sport to define your identity and how to maintain a healthy perspective.

The Dangers of Allowing Your Sport to Define Your Identity

When athletes allow their sport to define their identity, they can become overly invested in their sport and may place undue pressure on themselves to succeed. This pressure can lead to burnout and can have a negative impact on mental and emotional well-being. Furthermore, when athletes place their identity solely in their sport, they may experience feelings of emptiness and purposelessness when their sport career ends.

The Importance of Finding Your Own Identity

It is important for athletes to find their own identity outside of their sport. This can involve exploring new interests and hobbies, spending time with friends and family, or volunteering in their community. By finding their own identity, athletes can build resilience and find fulfillment in their lives, even in the face of challenges in their sport.

The Power of Positive Self-Talk

Positive self-talk can also play an important role in helping athletes maintain a healthy perspective and find their own identity outside of their sport. By speaking positively to themselves and focusing on their strengths and accomplishments, athletes can build confidence and resilience, and can maintain their well-being, even when faced with challenges in their sport.

In conclusion, it is important for athletes to remember that their sport does not define who they are as a person. By finding their own identity outside of their sport, speaking positively to themselves, and having a strong support system, athletes can maintain a healthy perspective and find fulfillment in their lives beyond their sport.

"Your sport is a part of your journey, but it is not your entire story. Embrace all that you are, beyond your sport, and never let it define your worth or your identity. You are more than an athlete, you are a unique and valuable human being with a rich tapestry of experiences, talents, and passions to explore."

Daniel Terry President/Founder

F.O.E.S Up Foundation

Chapter 5

When Plan A Should Be Plan B

Athletes Making Professional Sports #1 and Not Their Major in College

For many athletes, their goal is to turn their sport into a professional career. However, it is important to remember that not all athletes will reach this level of success, and it is crucial to have a backup plan in place. In this chapter, we will explore the dangers of making professional sports one's only plan and why it is important to have a Plan B.

The Risks of Making Professional Sports Plan A

When athletes make professional sports their only plan, they can put a great deal of pressure on themselves to succeed. This pressure can lead to burnout, injuries, and can have a negative impact on mental and emotional well-being.

Furthermore, many athletes may not reach the level of success they desire, which can lead to feelings of disappointment and frustration.

The Benefits of Having a Plan B

Having a Plan B can provide a safety net for athletes and can help reduce the pressure to succeed in their sport. This can involve pursuing a college degree or learning a new skill that can be applied outside of the sport. Having a backup plan can also provide a sense of purpose and fulfillment, even if the athlete's professional sport career does not pan out as planned.

The Importance of Preparing for Life After Sports

Preparing for life after sports is crucial for all athletes, regardless of whether they make it to the professional level or not. By having a Plan B in place, athletes can ensure that they have a meaningful and fulfilling life after their sport career ends.

In conclusion, while making professional sports Plan A may seem like the best option, it is important to remember that not all athletes will reach this level of success.

Having a Plan B in place can provide a sense of purpose, reduce pressure, and prepare athletes for life after sports.

Plan B Doesn't Mean You Don't Believe in Yourself

Many athletes may feel like having a Plan B means that they are not confident in their abilities or that they don't believe in themselves. However, this is not the case. Having a backup plan is simply a way of preparing for the future and ensuring that one has a fallback option if their primary plan does not work out.

Balancing Plan A and Plan B

Athletes should focus on balancing their Plan A and Plan B. This means putting in the necessary effort and hard work to pursue their professional sport career, while also preparing for life after sports. This can involve taking courses or workshops in a field that interests them, networking with individuals in that field, and gaining practical experience in their Plan B.

The Benefits of Balancing Plan A and Plan B

Balancing Plan A and Plan B can help athletes feel more secure and confident in their abilities. It can also provide a sense of purpose and fulfillment, even if their sport career does not pan out as planned. Furthermore, having a backup plan can help reduce the pressure to succeed in their sport, allowing athletes to perform at their best.

In conclusion, having a Plan B does not mean that athletes don't believe in themselves. Rather, it is a way of preparing for the future and ensuring that one has a fallback option if their primary plan does not work out. Balancing Plan A and Plan B can help athletes feel more secure, reduce pressure, and provide a sense of purpose and fulfillment.

> "Having a backup plan doesn't mean you don't believe in your abilities or your dreams. It means you believe in yourself enough to have a safety net, to be prepared for whatever the future may bring, and to have the confidence to chase your dreams without fear of failure." *Dejon Jernagin*

Chapter 6

Dealing with the Reminders of Past Success and Current Struggles

Dealing with the Reminders of Past Success and Current Struggles

For many athletes, depression can be triggered by reminders of their past success and the contrast with their current struggles. It can be difficult to reconcile the person they were with the person they are now, and this can lead to feelings of disappointment and worthlessness.

Facing the Reality

To deal with these feelings, it is important for athletes to face the reality of their situation and to understand that it is okay to not always be at their best. The road to success is rarely linear, and there will be ups and downs along the way.

Focus on the Present

Instead of dwelling on past successes or current struggles, athletes should focus on the present. This means setting achievable goals and taking small steps towards them. It also means embracing the process and learning from their experiences, both positive and negative.

Finding Support

Athletes can also find support from family, friends, and professionals. Talking to someone who understands and can offer guidance and encouragement can help athletes overcome their feelings of depression and regain their sense of self-worth.

In conclusion, dealing with reminders of past success and current struggles can be difficult for athletes struggling with depression. To overcome these feelings, it is important to face the reality of the situation, focus on the present, and find support from family, friends, and professionals. With the right tools and resources, athletes can regain their sense of self-worth and find hope for the future.

Regret is a common emotion for athletes who are struggling with depression. They may look back at their past decisions and wonder what could have been if they had chosen differently. This can lead to feelings of sadness, frustration, and anger, which can further exacerbate their depression.

Embracing the Past

One of the keys to overcoming regret is to embrace the past, both the good and the bad. Instead of focusing on what could have been, athletes should focus on what they learned from their experiences and how they can use those lessons to improve their future.

Forgiving Yourself

Another important step in overcoming regret is to forgive yourself. Athletes should understand that everyone makes mistakes and that it is okay to have regrets. It is also important to remember that the past cannot be changed and that the only thing they can control is the present and future.

Finding a New Purpose

Finally, athletes should find a new purpose in life. This could involve pursuing a new career, volunteering, or finding a new hobby. By finding something that they are passionate about and that gives them a sense of fulfillment, athletes can overcome their feelings of regret and depression and start to see the future in a more positive light.

In conclusion, overcoming regret is an important step in the journey towards overcoming depression for athletes. By embracing the past, forgiving themselves, and finding a new purpose in life, athletes can start to see the future in a more positive light and find hope for a better tomorrow.

> "Regret is a heavy burden to bear, but it is one that can be lifted with self-forgiveness and a focus on the future. Remember, the past has already happened and what's done is done. Embrace your experiences, learn from them, and use them to shape a brighter future. Remember Romans 8:1."
>
> *Dejon Jernagin*

Chapter 7

A New Mindset and Moving Beyond the Cheers

For athletes who have struggled with depression, the road to recovery often begins with a change in mindset. This means letting go of old habits and beliefs that may have been holding them back, and embracing a new way of thinking that is more positive and empowering.

Breaking Free from the Past

One of the biggest obstacles to recovery is the pull of the past. Athletes may find themselves constantly thinking about their past successes and failures, and this can prevent them from moving forward and finding happiness in the present. In order to break free from the past, athletes need to focus on the present moment and look ahead to the future.

Moving Beyond the Cheers

Another important aspect of a new mindset is moving beyond the cheers. For many athletes, the adulation and recognition that comes with success is a big part of what drives them. However, when the cheers stop and the recognition fades, athletes may find themselves feeling lost and empty. In order to move beyond the cheers, athletes need to focus on their own personal fulfillment and happiness, rather than seeking external validation from others.

Finding Inner Strength

Finally, a new mindset means tapping into one's inner strength. Athletes must recognize that they are stronger than they think, and that they have the ability to overcome their depression and find happiness again. This requires a shift in focus, from external validation to self-discovery and self-love. In conclusion, a new mindset is essential for athletes who are struggling with depression.

By breaking free from the past, moving beyond the cheers, and tapping into their inner strength, athletes can find the hope and happiness they need to move forward and lead fulfilling lives.

The Cheers as an Addiction

For many athletes, the cheers and recognition that come with success can be addictive. The adrenaline rush and sense of accomplishment that comes from performing well can be highly addictive, and athletes may find themselves constantly seeking that feeling of excitement and validation. However, when the cheers stop, athletes can find themselves in a dark place. They may feel lost and disconnected, and this can lead to feelings of depression and anxiety. This is why it is so important for athletes to recognize that their addiction to the cheers is not healthy, and that they need to find new sources of happiness and fulfillment.

Breaking the Cycle

Breaking free from the cycle of addiction to the cheers is not easy, but it is possible. Athletes need to be proactive in finding new ways to engage with the world, and new sources of happiness and validation. This may mean taking up a new hobby, volunteering, or simply spending more time with friends and family. In addition, athletes need to be honest with themselves about why they are seeking the cheers in the first place. Are they looking for validation from others, or are they trying to fill a void in their lives? Understanding the root causes of their addiction can help athletes find more healthy and sustainable ways to feel fulfilled and happy.

Finding Inner Strength

Ultimately, breaking free from the addiction to the cheers requires tapping into one's inner strength. Athletes must recognize that they are stronger than they think, and that they have the power to find happiness and fulfillment without relying on the cheers. This requires a shift in focus, from external validation to self-discovery and self-love.

In conclusion, recognizing that the cheers are an addiction and breaking free from that cycle is essential for athletes who are struggling with depression. By finding new sources of happiness, understanding the root causes of their addiction, and tapping into their inner strength, athletes can find the hope and happiness they need to move forward and lead fulfilling lives.

"True success is not determined by the cheers, but by the strength and resilience of the human spirit."

Chapter 8

Embracing the New You And New Journey

Embracing the New You and New Journey

For many athletes, the end of their sporting career can be a time of great change and uncertainty. They may feel as though they have lost their identity and purpose, and this can lead to feelings of depression and anxiety.

However, it is important to remember that this new chapter in life presents a unique opportunity for growth and self-discovery. Athletes must embrace the new person they are becoming and the new journey they are embarking on.

Finding a New Purpose

One of the key steps in embracing the new journey is to find a new purpose. Athletes must identify what they are passion-

-ate about, what makes them happy, and what they want to achieve in life. This could be a new career, a new hobby, or a new way of giving back to their community.

By focusing on their new purpose, athletes can find a sense of meaning and fulfillment, which can help them overcome feelings of depression and anxiety.

Embracing New Challenges

Another important aspect of embracing the new journey is to embrace new challenges. Athletes must be willing to take risks, step outside of their comfort zones, and face new challenges head-on.

This can help athletes develop new skills, gain new experiences, and grow as individuals. In addition, facing new challenges can be a great source of confidence, as athletes learn that they are capable of much more than they previously thought.

Learning to Embrace the New You

Finally, it is important for athletes to learn to embrace the new person they are becoming. This requires letting go of the past, accepting their new identity, and focusing on the present and future.

By embracing the new person they are becoming, athletes can find a sense of peace and acceptance, which can help them move forward and lead fulfilling lives.

In conclusion, embracing the new journey and new person can be a challenging and transformative process, but it is essential for athletes who are struggling with depression. By finding a new purpose, embracing new challenges, and embracing the new person they are becoming, athletes can find the hope and happiness they need to move forward and lead fulfilling lives.

The Process of Discovery

Athletes must remember that their new journey should not be approached with the same level of intensity and pressure as their athletic career. Instead, they must focus on enjoying the process of discovery and giving the new venture all they've got, even more so than they did in their athletic career.

This means taking things one step at a time, being patient, and not being afraid to make mistakes. It is important to remember that the new journey is just that, a journey, and not a destination. Finding balance and taking care of oneself should also be a priority. This means setting aside time for self-care activities such as exercise, reading, meditating, or spending time with friends and family.

Encountering new experiences, meeting new people, and learning new things can be exciting and invigorating. Embracing this new chapter in life with a positive attitude and open mind can lead to a newfound sense of purpose, happiness, and fulfillment.

In short, by giving the new journey more than what was given to the sport and by embracing the process of discovery, athletes can find a new and meaningful path forward. They can overcome feelings of depression, and find a renewed sense of purpose, happiness, and fulfillment.

> "Success is not just about the destination, it's about the journey. Embrace the new with an open mind, and you will find a path to happiness and fulfillment."

In the next chapter, we'll discuss the importance of athletes to understand that it is okay to continue watching their former sport and be around former successful players. Keeping up with the sport and former teammates can provide a sense of nostalgia and comfort, reminding them of their past achievements and glory days.

However, it is important for athletes to also find a healthy balance in their relationship with their former sport. It is not uncommon for athletes to experience feelings of frustration or sadness when they watch their former sport, especially if they are no longer able to participate at the same level. In these cases, it may be helpful to limit exposure to the sport and focus on other interests and activities.

Additionally, being around former successful players can also bring up feelings of comparison and competition, leading to negative self-talk and a decrease in self-esteem. It is important for athletes to understand that everyone has their own journey and to not compare themselves to others.

In conclusion, while it is okay to watch your former sport and be around former successful players, it is important to find a healthy balance in the relationship and to not let it negatively impact one's mental health.

In Chapter 9

Destroying Bitterness

It is also important for athletes to recognize and overcome bitterness that may arise from their athletic experiences. Bitterness can stem from a variety of sources such as feeling unfulfilled in their athletic careers, facing injury or setbacks, or feeling like they did not receive the recognition they deserved.

It is important for athletes to understand that holding onto bitterness can have a negative impact on their mental and emotional wellbeing. Bitterness can prevent individuals from moving forward and finding joy in other aspects of their lives.

To overcome bitterness, athletes can try the following strategies:

1. Reframe their perspective: Try to focus on the positive experiences and memories that came from their athletic careers instead of dwelling on the negative aspects.

2. Find closure: If there is an issue or situation that is causing bitterness, try to find closure by talking to the individuals involved or seeking therapy.

3. Embrace change: Recognize that life is constantly changing and that it is okay to move on from their athletic careers and embrace new challenges and opportunities.

4. Seek support: Surround yourself with friends, family, or a support group who can provide encouragement and support during this transition.

In conclusion, it is important for athletes to recognize and overcome bitterness in order to move forward and find happiness in other aspects of their lives.

"Bitterness may try to hold you back, but remember that it is only as strong as the grip you give it. Let go of the bitterness and embrace the new journey ahead."

"Remember, the past is behind us, but it does not have to define us. Embrace your new journey and let the memories of your past athletic achievements serve as a source of inspiration and encouragement."

Chapter 10

The End Is Not the End. It's the Beginning

It is important for athletes to understand that just because their athletic careers have ended, it does not mean that their journey is over. There is still so much more that they can do and achieve, regardless of their age.

It is important for athletes to remember that their athletic careers have equipped them with valuable skills and qualities such as discipline, dedication, and teamwork, which they can apply to other areas of their lives.

They can also pursue new passions and interests, and use their experiences to help others who are facing similar challenges.

For some athletes, their athletic careers may have ended prematurely due to injury or other circumstances, but it is important to not let this discourage them. They can still find fulfillment and purpose in other areas of their lives and make a positive impact in the world.

It is also important for athletes to understand that they are not alone in their journey. There are many other athletes who have gone through similar experiences and have found success and happiness in other areas of their lives.

The 18 year old thinks it's ended but in reality, it is just the beginning it is important for young athletes to understand that even if their athletic careers may have ended at a young age, it is not the end. They still have so much potential and so much life ahead of them.

It is important for young athletes to not let their athletic careers define them and to instead focus on their education and personal growth. They can explore new interests and passions, and develop skills that will benefit them in their future endeavors.

For some young athletes, their athletic careers may have ended prematurely due to injury or other circumstances, but it is important for them to not let this discourage them. Instead, they should use this as an opportunity to grow and to learn new things.

It is also important for young athletes to understand that they are not alone in their journey. There are many resources and support systems available to help them navigate this transition and to find success and happiness in other areas of their lives.

The 18 year old thinks it's ended but in reality, it is just the beginning. It is important for young athletes to understand that even if their athletic careers may have ended at a young age, it is not the end. They still have so much potential and so much life ahead of them.

It is important for young athletes to not let their athletic careers define them and to instead focus on their education and personal growth. They can explore new interests and passions, and develop skills that will benefit them in their future endeavors.

For some young athletes, their athletic careers may have ended prematurely due to injury or other circumstances, but it is important for them to not let this discourage them. Instead, they should use this as an opportunity to grow and to learn new things.

It is also important for young athletes to understand that they are not alone in their journey. There are many resources and support systems available to help them navigate this transition and to find success and happiness in other areas of their lives.

> "Age is just a number, it is never too late to start a new journey and make a positive impact in the world. Embrace your experiences and continue to grow, no matter how old you are."

"The end of your athletic career at 18 may seem like the end, but in reality, it is just the beginning. Embrace the new journey and use your experiences to make a positive impact in the world."

"The end of your athletic career does not mean the end of your journey. It is just the beginning of a new chapter, where you can write your own story and make a positive impact in the world."

Final Thoughts From Dejon Jernagin:

When The Cheers Stopped I looked for more cheers and it hurt until I cheered for myself.

"When the cheers stopped and the lights turned off on my athletic career, I was left feeling lost and unsure of what to do next. But as I continued down my journey, I learned that the greatest cheerleader I could have was myself. I had to find joy and fulfillment in my own accomplishments, rather than relying on the applause of others.

It was a difficult transition, but I am so grateful for the lessons I learned along the way. I hope that by sharing my story in this book, I can inspire others to find their own inner strength and to never give up on their dreams, no matter what obstacles they may face.

So when the cheers stop, don't be afraid to start cheering for yourself. You are capable of greatness and your journey is far from over."

Here are ten things that athletes can do to get through depression:

1. Seek professional help: Talk to a licensed therapist or counselor who has experience working with athletes to help you develop coping strategies and manage your depression.

2. Practice self-care: Take care of your body and mind by getting enough sleep, eating a healthy diet, and engaging in activities that you enjoy.

3. Stay active: Exercise is a powerful tool for managing depression. Make time for regular physical activity and find a sport or activity that you love.

4. Connect with others: Reach out to friends, family, coaches, or teammates for support and understanding.

5. Set achievable goals: Identify small goals that you can work towards and celebrate each accomplishment along the way.

6. Engage in mindfulness and meditation: Mindfulness and meditation can help reduce stress and improve your overall well-being.

7. Get outside: Spending time in nature can help improve your mood and reduce stress levels.

8. Challenge negative thoughts: Learn to recognize negative thoughts and challenge them with positive self-talk.

9. Find purpose: Identify the things in life that give you a sense of purpose and work towards incorporating them into your daily routine.

10. Take time for yourself: Take time each day to relax and unwind. This can include activities like reading a book, taking a bath, or practicing yoga.

Dedications

To Harvey Jernagin, my father and hero, for teaching me the importance of hard work, determination, and perseverance. Your unwavering love and support have been my guiding light through every challenge I have faced.

To Shellee Jernagin, my wife, for always being there for me through thick and thin. Your love, encouragement, and understanding have been my rock through every high and low.

To Isaiah, Isaac, and Ian, my sons, for allowing me to coach you and for inspiring me every day with your passion and determination. You have shown me what it means to be a true champion.

To my mother, Janet Hammond, for instilling in me the values of faith, courage, and resilience. Your love and support have been the foundation of my life.

To my grandmothers, Ernestine Holland and Ruby Jernagin, for their unwavering love and support throughout my life. Your wisdom and guidance have been my compass in life.

To Candice Jernagin, my sister, who has been a constant source of encouragement and inspiration.

To my Aunt Regina Hanks, and cousins Toni Roberson, Jasmine and Jamal Simpkins who are forever supportive.

And to my Uncle Eddie Ransom, my other hero, who was my first example of an athlete and taught me the importance of perseverance and dedication.

To Pastor Howard Swancy, who has provided guidance and support through my spiritual journey;

To Coach Craig Noyes, who has taught me the importance of hard work and perseverance;

This book is dedicated to all of you, for your love, support and encouragement--the driving force behind my success.

Contact Information

To contact Mr. Jernagin, order more copies of this book, or to arrange a speaking engagement, call or click today.

Email: dejonjernagin@yahoo.com
Website: www.themanupfoundation.org

Facebook:
https://www.facebook.com/dejonthedeacon.jernagin

Mailing: The Man Up Foundation
1929 Truxton Avenue
Bakersfield, CA 93301

Made in the USA
Columbia, SC
27 March 2025

55761869R00041